How to Start, Grow Your Own Business and Be Successful: Easy Steps to Start Your Own Business, Make Money and Achieve Success

Vincent M. Lester

About the author

Vincent M. Lester, a luminary in the world of business, brings a wealth of entrepreneurial experience and a proven track record of success to the forefront. With a career spanning decades, Vincent has etched his name as a dynamic and visionary businessman, leaving an indelible mark on various industries.

Entrepreneurial Odyssey: A Journey of Triumphs and Lessons

Vincent's entrepreneurial journey is a tapestry woven with triumphs, challenges, and invaluable lessons. From the inception of his first venture to steering multimillion-dollar enterprises, he has navigated the complex terrain of business with acumen and resilience. His diverse experiences have not only honed his strategic thinking but have also instilled a deep understanding of the ever-evolving dynamics of the business world.

Architect of Success: Building and Growing Businesses

As a seasoned architect of success, Vincent has not only built businesses from the ground up but has also orchestrated their growth into formidable entities. His ventures stand as a testament to his ability to identify opportunities, navigate market fluctuations, and lead teams toward sustainable success. Whether in traditional sectors or the dynamic realm of digital entrepreneurship, Vincent's innovative spirit has been a guiding force.

Mentor and Thought Leader: Sharing Wisdom

Vincent M. Lester is not just a businessman; he is a mentor and thought leader committed to sharing the wisdom garnered from his extensive journey. Through mentorship programs, keynote speeches, and contributions to business publications, Vincent empowers aspiring entrepreneurs to think strategically, embrace resilience, and chart their course toward success.

Diverse Industry Footprints: A Legacy of Excellence

Vincent's influence spans a spectrum of industries, from traditional brick-and-mortar establishments to cutting-edge ventures in the digital landscape. His ability to adapt to changing market landscapes and harness the power of innovation has positioned him as a driving force behind the success of businesses across diverse sectors.

Authorship: A Chronicle of Insights

In addition to his thriving business ventures, Vincent M. Lester is a prolific author, sharing his insights and expertise with a global audience. His writings encapsulate a pragmatic blend of business acumen, leadership principles, and the art of navigating challenges. Through his authored works, Vincent invites readers into the corridors of his experiences, offering practical wisdom for those embarking on their entrepreneurial odyssey.

Vincent's Vision for the Future:

Vincent continues to be a visionary force, steering businesses toward new horizons and inspiring the next generation of entrepreneurs. His commitment to excellence, coupled with a passion for innovation, paints a compelling picture of a businessman whose legacy is not just in the success of his ventures but in the knowledge shared and the lives impacted along the way.

As you delve into the pages crafted by Vincent M. Lester, be prepared to embark on a journey of entrepreneurial enlightenment—a journey illuminated by the experiences, triumphs, and profound insights of a true business luminary.

Table of contents

Introduction

Welcome to "How to Start, Grow Your Own Business and Be Successful." In the unique scene of business, leaving on the excursion to construct and maintain your own business is both thrilling and testing. This book fills in as your compass, directing you through the fundamental standards and functional advances expected to send off your endeavor as well as flourish in the serious business world.

As we explore the parts ahead, we'll investigate the critical components of business venture, from developing the right outlook and creating a strong marketable strategy to figuring out the elements of securing clients, tackling the force of online stages, and exploring the complexities of funding your endeavor.Whether you're an old pro hoping to take an intense action or a newbie anxious to transform an energy into a maintainable business, this guide is custom fitted to furnish you with the information and instruments fundamental for progress.

Thus, we should leave on this groundbreaking excursion together, where development meets commitment, and where your innovative desires can advance into a prospering and versatile business. Prepare to reveal the mysteries of effective business and set up for your own victorious endeavor.

• Setting the Stage for Entrepreneurial Success

In the tremendous domain of enterprising undertakings, achievement frequently tracks down its foundations in the rich soil of cautious planning and a distinct vision. Before you leave on the elating excursion of going into business, making way for enterprising success is significant.

Developing the Right Mentality:

The underpinning of innovative achievement starts with your mentality. Embrace an outlook that flourishes with development, strength, and flexibility. Comprehend that difficulties are unavoidable yet view them as any open doors for development.

Explaining Your Vision:

An effective endeavor is based on a reasonable and convincing vision. Get some margin to verbalize what your business does as well as why it exists. Your vision will act as a directing light, controlling your choices and activities.

Making Reasonable Objectives:

Put forth feasible and quantifiable objectives that line up with your vision. These objectives will give a guide, permitting you to follow progress and celebrate achievements en route. Separate bigger targets into more modest, reasonable advances.

Embracing the Excursion:

Perceive that the pioneering venture is a dynamic and developing interaction. Be available to gain from encounters, whether they are victories or mishaps. Adaptability and a readiness to adjust will be your partners.

Building an Emotionally supportive network:

Encircle yourself with an organization of help. Look for direction from coaches, interface with individual business people, and draw in with networks pertinent to your industry. The aggregate insight and support can be significant.

Making way for pioneering achievement is definitely not a one-size-fits-all undertaking; it's a customized, purposeful exertion that lays the basis for what lies ahead. As you set out on this way, recollect that each step is a structure block, and with a strong groundwork, your innovative excursion can thrive.

● Overview of the Book's Purpose and Structure

This book, "How to Start, Grow Your Own Business and Be Successful,"is planned as an extensive manual for engaging hopeful business people with the information and instruments expected to explore the difficult yet compensating scene of business proprietorship. We should investigate the reason and design that support this keen excursion.

Reason for the Book:

The essential point of this book is to demystify the intricacies of business ventures and give reasonable bits of knowledge that impel you towards progress. Whether you're moving into the business world or trying to refine your methodology, this guide is custom fitted to offer direction, motivation, and significant techniques.

Exploring Innovative Fundamentals:

Every section tends to key components significant for innovative achievement. From understanding the outlook of fruitful business visionaries to creating a hearty field-tested strategy, characterizing your exceptional incentive, and excelling at securing clients, the book unfurls a bit by bit guide.

Viable and Noteworthy Bits of knowledge:

Instead of overpowering you with hypothetical ideas, this book underlines common sense, genuine applications. Expect noteworthy hints, contextual investigations, and activities that urge you to apply the standards talked about, transforming information into substantial advancement.

Organized Learning Excursion:

The book is organized in a consistent grouping, beginning with basic ideas like outlook and arranging, advancing through the phases of business improvement, and coming full circle in cutting edge points like development, transformation, and development. This organized methodology guarantees a comprehensive comprehension of the innovative excursion.

Empowering Reflection and Application:

All through the book, you'll track down snapshots of reflection, empowering you to apply the ideas to your one of a kind business setting. Whether it's putting forth objectives, refining your business thought, or adjusting techniques, these minutes brief you to customize the experiences acquired.

As you leave on this understanding experience, imagine it as a unique discussion — your side through the complexities of business venture. The intention isn't simply to grant information however to engage you to make sure strides towards building and supporting an effective business. Thus, we should make a plunge and investigate the extraordinary universe of innovative accomplishment together.

Chapter1:Think Like an Entrepreneur

Thinking like an entrepreneur implies freeing yourself up to an innovative mentality. It goes past simply beginning a business — it's a one of a kind approach to moving toward difficulties, open doors, and life itself. A pioneering outlook is a perspective described by development, versatility, vision, and a determined quest for transforming thoughts into the real world. A disposition embraces risk, searches out arrangements, and is driven by an energy for making worth and having a beneficial outcome on the world.

Instructions to concoct innovative thoughts

1. Be conscious about tracking down the following good thoughts. Try not to trust that motivation will come to you. Great data makes for good motivation, so focus in and assemble the data you really want to pursue a sound choice.

2. The following are three hints about how business people recognize new business open doors:

3. Begin with what you definitely know. Your mastery can be a major advantage, so start searching for business thoughts contacting things you definitely know how to do.

4. Contemplate what items or administrations you wish existed. There is no such thing as in the event that they consider what it would take to make them a reality.

5. Research what other fruitful business people have tried.Sometimes it's tied in with having the perfect thought brilliantly. This moment may be the opportunity for a thought that came too early for another person.

How business visionaries recognize new business valuable open doors

1. Creating pioneering thoughts is the initial step, however distinguishing suitable business open doors is the way to progress. To decide whether your thoughts can possibly become productive endeavors, you want to assess them basically and proficiently. Here are reasonable moves toward quickly evaluate the feasibility of your pioneering thoughts:

2. Direct statistical surveying. Prior to jumping into any business thought, perform careful statistical surveying.

Figure out your interest group and their requirements, inclinations, and trouble spots. Search for holes in the market that your thought could fill or potential chances to work on existing items or administrations. Statistical surveying gives significant experiences into request, contest, and likely clients, assisting you with settling on informed conclusions about chasing after a specific thought.

3. Think about practicality and scalability.Evaluate the plausibility of transforming your thought into a feasible business. Survey the assets required, like funds, abilities, and innovation. Moreover, think about the versatility of your thought — does it have the potential for development and extension? A versatile thought can draw in financial backers and lead to long haul achievement.

4. Investigate rivalry and industry patterns. Comprehend your opposition and industry patterns. Investigate what comparative organizations are offering, their assets, shortcomings, and market situating. Recognizing holes in the opposition can introduce amazing open doors for separation and development.

5. Evaluate market timing. Timing can altogether influence the outcome of a thought. Evaluate whether the market is prepared for your item or administration. In some cases, a thought might have been relatively radical already, yet the ongoing economic situations might be better for its prosperity now. Watch out for arising patterns and changing buyer ways of behaving that could line up with your thoughts.

6. Look for mentorship and advice.Connect with experienced

business visionaries or industry specialists who can offer direction and guidance. They might give significant bits of knowledge, share their own encounters, and assist you with exploring possible difficulties.

7. Stay open to transformation. Be ready to adjust and turn if vital. Beginning thoughts might require acclimations to line up with market requests or evolving conditions. Adaptability and receptiveness to change can prompt effective business open doors.

Benefits of thinking like an entrepreneur.

Thinking like a business person offers many benefits that reach out past the domain of business. Whether applied to your expert life or individual undertakings, embracing an innovative attitude can prompt amazing development and satisfaction. Here are the vital advantages of reasoning like a business visionary in a business setting.

- Development and inventiveness. An enterprising attitude cultivates advancement and innovativeness, empowering you to foster extraordinary arrangements and remain in front of the opposition.
- Opportunity acknowledgment. You'll become proficient at spotting business potential open doors, recognizing holes on the lookout, and exploiting arising patterns.
- Versatility and resilience.Entrepreneurs are talented at exploring difficulties, adjusting to evolving conditions, and returning quickly from misfortunes, guaranteeing the drawn out manageability of their endeavors.
- Client driven approach. By focusing on client needs, you'll construct more grounded connections, draw in a

faithful customer base, and drive business development through sure verbal.

- Risk the executives. Thinking like a business visionary implies determined risk-taking, where you figure out how to evaluate and oversee dangers to streamline results and make progress.
- Business development and extension. A pioneering mentality supports aspiration and vital preparation, making ready for business development, broadening, and extension.

• Understanding the Entrepreneurial Mindset

What is an entrepreneurial mindset?

Entrepreneurial mindset: a perspective that empowers you to defeat difficulties, be definitive, and acknowledge liability regarding your results. You should continually work on your abilities, gain from your mix-ups, and follow up on your thoughts. Anybody put in the effort can foster a pioneering mentality.

Five characteristics of an entrepreneurial mindset

Many qualities define the mindset of an entrepreneur. Here are probably the most unmistakable ones:

1. Freedom

Independent learning is important to accomplish any objective, whether private or expert. You're your best team promoter and your best resource when the opportunity arrives to act.

It's wise to cooperate with others and get support from the people who can give it. However, a specific degree of freedom and confidence in your own capacities is important to continue to push ahead.

2. Responsibility

Taking responsibility for wins and mistakes is a characteristic of any great business person. This enables you and permits you to think about what your activities mean for yourself as well as other people, what you've gained from your mix-ups, and all that you've achieved.

3. Objective situated

The best business visionaries are engaged people who focus on their objectives and follow an activity situated direction to accomplish them. Understanding what you believe you should do is the initial step to making progress.

4. Flexibility

Slip-ups and disappointments go with the job of facing challenges and having a pioneering soul. Returning and pushing ahead regardless of difficulties and difficulty will assist you with developing, learning, and construct your critical thinking range of abilities.

5. Readiness to analyze

Leaving nothing to chance, however a strong choice, just takes you up to this point. Individuals with an innovative mentality don't avoid disappointment.

In any event, when trials don't have ideal results, it's as yet significant. Trying out various field-tested strategies or the executives' techniques, gathering input, and pursuing difficult choices are each of the pieces of this cycle. Here and there you want to know when to move your concentration to one more task or point you hadn't considered previously.

How to develop an entrepreneurial mindset

Anyone can cultivate the right mindset. Searching out similar people, new pursuits, and encounters and proceeding to develop your insight into this specific domain is an extraordinary spot to start.

Here is a rundown of tips to assist you with fostering an innovative outlook:

1. Put forth clear objectives

Showing your fantasies on paper or without holding back can be the flash you want to begin. Framing where you intend to go can go about as a visual indication of your objectives. It can likewise urge you to think about your achievements and bearing. These objectives could apply to your business, vocation, or individual life. Innovative achievement ordinarily applies to entrepreneurs, yet your enterprising abilities will help any of your aspirations.

2. Work on being conclusive

Business visionaries, understudies, guardians, and in the middle between should pursue choices everyday. It's everything except compulsory fundamental ability. On the off chance that you can't decide, you won't gain ground. Luckily, it's a simple undertaking to rehearse — you can begin little, such as requesting at an eatery, and afterward move gradually up to huge minutes.

3. Reclassify disappointment

You can't stay away from disappointment, and life is brimming with them. The best anyone can hope for at this point is to deal with difficulties directly and transform them into opportunities for growth. While it requires investment, displaying a cognizant work to modify your outlook will emphatically help you over the long haul. Mental health will work on your presentation and lead to confidence, and you'll fail to remember what disappointment at any point implied.

4. Confront your apprehensions

Dread is unavoidable in your expert and individual life. Drawing in with circumstances beyond your usual range of familiarity assists you with developing. Tending to and investigating what concerns you will draw you one stage nearer to accomplishing your objectives. Keep in mind: weakness is solid.

5. Stay inquisitive

Allow your internal identity to run free and wonderous. Continuously be interested about your opposition, latest things and occasions, new advances, new individuals, and new business thoughts. Pursue online courses and pay attention to digital recordings about your industry. In a flash, you'll be among the fruitful organizations you've caught wind of.

• Embracing Creativity and Vision

Sustaining Your Pioneering Creative mind

Consider innovativeness and vision the unique team that shapes the spirit of business venture — your own enchanted wand for transforming dreams into the real world. In this part, we'll investigate the charming domains of imagination and visionary reasoning, opening the ways to development and the specialty of making a significant future.

Taking advantage of Your Imaginative Stream:

Inventiveness is your mystery ingredient, the unique fixing that makes your business stick out. It's tied in with allowing your creative mind to roam free, addressing standards, and tracking down brilliant arrangements. Imagine yourself as a craftsman, and your endeavor as a material sitting tight for your exceptional strokes.

The Force of Vision:

Your vision is your compass, pointing towards the objective of accomplishment. It's about where you are as well as where you're going. Embrace the capacity to imagine a future that energizes you, adjusting your activities to the 10,000 foot view to direct your enterprising excursion.

Stares off into space and Enormous Dreams:

Allow your psyche to meander. Wandering off in fantasy land isn't an interruption; it's a jungle gym for your enterprising creative mind. Permit yourself to think beyond practical boundaries, to envision the incomprehensible. It's inside these fantasies that you could track down the seeds of your next momentous thought.

Transforming Difficulties into Wins:

Innovativeness assists you with seeing difficulties as riddles ready to be addressed. Rather than getting hindered, view obstacles as solicitations for advancement. Embrace the possibility that each issue is an open door in camouflage, an opportunity to grandstand your imaginative critical thinking ability.

Carrying Human Touch with Configuration Thinking:

Envision your clients as companions you profoundly care about. Configuration thinking, at its center, is tied in with figuring out their requirements, relating to their battles, and creating arrangements that work as well as reverberate inwardly. About making items and encounters individuals really love.

Encouraging an Inventive People group:

Similarly as a craftsman flourishes in an energetic local area, business people prosper in conditions that energize imagination. Construct a group that values different viewpoints, embraces trial and error, and sees disappointment not as a mishap but rather as a venturing stone toward progress.

Thus, as you set out on this imaginative odyssey, recollect that you're not simply beginning a business; you're making a story, a story where innovativeness and vision are your heroes. Allow your creative mind to take off, and let your vision guide you toward a future that mirrors the brightness of your enterprising soul. This is your excursion — make it a magnum opus.

Chapter 2:How to Get Started

Getting everything rolling: Transforming Dreams right into it

Going into business is an outright exhilarating undertaking, yet the way from dream to reality requires key preparation and intentional activity. In this section, we'll separate the fundamental stages to assist you with progressing from hopeful business visionary to dynamic entrepreneur.

Getting everything rolling is tied in with making an interpretation of your pioneering vision into substantial advances. Each activity carries you nearer to your objective. Keep in mind, the excursion might appear to be overwhelming on occasion, however making these underlying strides establishes the groundwork for an effective and satisfying endeavor. In this way, put pen to paper, sketch out your arrangement, and take that first step toward transforming your business dreams into the real world.

• Setting Clear Goals and Objectives

Five ways to set clear goals and objectives

Fostering a marketable strategy is fundamental for the progress of any business, however laying out clear objectives and goals is critical to making that progress. A marketable strategy that needs unambiguous and quantifiable objectives is just an assortment of thoughts and desires. To make a strong starting point for your business, it's essential to define clear objectives and goals that line up with your vision for the organization.

Make Your Objectives Explicit and Quantifiable

The most important phase in laying out clear objectives and targets is to make them explicit and quantifiable. This implies that your objectives ought to be distinct and definite, and there ought to be a reasonable method for estimating progress and achievement. For instance, an overall objective like "increment income" isn't sufficiently explicit. A more unambiguous objective may be "increment income by 10%

in the following quarter." This objective is explicit, quantifiable, and gives a reasonable objective to pursue.

Adjust Your Objectives to Your Business Technique

The second way to set clear objectives and goals is to guarantee they line up with your business procedure. Your objectives ought to help your general vision for the business and ought to be in accordance with the methodologies you have created to accomplish that vision. For instance, on the off chance that your business methodology is to increment a piece of the pie, your objectives ought to mirror this system, like expanding deals or venturing into new business sectors.

Include Your Group in Objective Setting

The third way to set clear objectives and targets is to include your group in the objective setting process. By including your group, you make a feeling of pride and responsibility for accomplishing the objectives. Also, your colleagues might have important bits of knowledge and points of view that can assist you with putting forth more powerful objectives. At the point when representatives feel like they have something to do with the objectives of the business, they are bound to put resources into accomplishing them.

Put forth Reasonable and Attainable Objectives

The fourth way to set clear objectives and targets is to lay out practical and reachable objectives. Objectives that are too aggressive or unreasonable can be demotivating, while objectives that are too simple may not challenge your group enough. While defining objectives, think about your assets, capacities, and outer factors, for example, economic situations. It would be ideal for objectives to be tested, yet feasible. This makes a feeling of achievement and gathers speed towards accomplishing more huge targets.

Foster an Activity Plan for Accomplishing Your Objectives

The fifth and last way to set clear objectives and targets is to foster an activity plan for accomplishing your objectives. Your activity plan ought to frame the particular advances you will take to accomplish your objectives and the timetable for finishing those means. It ought to likewise recognize any expected obstructions and how you will defeat them. As indicated by Brad, fostering an activity plan is fundamental for accomplishing your objectives. This plan gives a guide to how you will accomplish your targets and guarantees that you are doing whatever it takes to contact them. Moreover, an activity plan assists with distinguishing any potential issues from the get-go, permitting you to address them before they become significant road obstructions to progress.

• Developing a Business Plan

Figuring out how to compose a strategy not just prompts an extraordinary diagram for running an organization, it compels you to look hard and long at how your business should be run. It can likewise be an "agenda" for guaranteeing your organization gets in good shape — monetarily and primarily.

Ordinarily, strategies fall into two classes: Conventional strategies and "lean startup" field-tested strategies.

- Customary strategies: This sort of field-tested strategy is complete and intensive — a "bit by bit" assessment of what's really going on with your organization and what it brings to the commercial center. A customary marketable strategy can be many pages long.
- Lean new company designs: This kind of strategy is a simple picture, stressing

the central issues about your business. A lean new company plan is much of the time a projectile pointed record that is just a single page long.

Decisively, it could be ideal to utilize your lean new company plan as an attempt to seal the deal to get lenders intrigued by your organization. Whenever you've stood out for them, then, at that point, circle back to the more definite, customary marketable strategy.

A Step-By-Step Guide to Creating a Business Plan

Follow these moves toward composing a marketable strategy that meets your organization's interesting necessities.

Stage 1: Chief Synopsis

This initial segment launches your field-tested strategy and momentarily frames the central issues of your arrangement. The objective here is to make sense of what your organization does and why it will find success. Incorporate an organization statement of purpose (i.e., what your definitive objective is as a business — in a sentence or two.)

Stage 2: Business Portrayal

This segment begins the fundamental part of your field-tested strategy. In it, you'll meticulously describe the situation of what your organization does, and what arrangements it will bring to the commercial center. In this segment, now is the ideal time to get explicit and detail what item or administrations you're creating and what clients you're focusing on. Incorporate a short history of your organization and notice any high level ability you have on board to get your organization going.

Stage 3: Market Investigation

In this segment, you'll detail the commercial center you'll contend in. Where could the best open doors in your market be? What is the commercial center? Who are your rivals? What are their assets and shortcomings? What is the main commercial center item or administration, and how are you enhancing the main items or administrations? Supporting organizations need to work with differentiators, and they'll need to understand which isolates your business from the pack. Here is the spot to tell them precisely that.

Stage 4: Organization Association

How might your organization work (i.e., as an organization or as an enterprise, fundamentally), and who will be the key leaders? How might the organization be organized lawfully? What is the administration ordered progression? Who has responsibility for organization and at which rate? These are the essential inquiries you'll have to respond to in the organization association segment of your marketable strategy.

Stage 5: Items or Administrations Gave

What will your organization produce, and how might it help clients? What sort of innovative work have you previously placed into your organization and what results would you say you are getting — and anticipating? Additionally, how might you showcase your item or administration to clients? These are the issues you'll have to reply to in this part.

Stage 6: Monetary Viewpoint

In this part, you'll have to spread out your monetary projections for your organization. Assuming your organization is now ready to go, list any pay explanations and income numbers for the beyond quite a while, if conceivable. Do you have any exceptional advances? What does your accounting report resemble? What are your quarterly projections proceeding? Organization funders consider this the main segment of your marketable strategy, so be careful and as exact as conceivable in introducing monetary information to your perusers — they'll be pouring over each word and each digit to judge regardless of whether there's a decent business opportunity here.

Stage 7: Synopsis

Close your field-tested strategy with a pitch for financing, and rundown any supporting information, diagrams, and graphs that reinforce your pitch. Clarify what you're searching for monetarily from lenders — value, an association, or a credit. Give a rough approximation of the subsidizing you want and clarify whether you're available to a discussion. An organization that knows how much cash it requires will be treated in a serious way by funders and lenders.

Tips on Writing Your Best Business Plan

The best marketable strategies cover the most ground at all measures of time. Go for the gold "C's" in fostering your field-tested strategy — give clarity , be concise and be convincing.

Raise a ruckus around town straightforwardly with these tips:

Find a Decent Field-tested strategy Diagram

There's actually a compelling reason to begin your field-tested strategy without any preparation. Utilize a strong web-based marketable strategy like LivePlan, which strolls you through the production of your whole strategy.

Track down Genuine Models and Stick to Their Style

Find extraordinary instances of industry-explicit field-tested strategies at online destinations like Bplans or LivePlan.com.

Root Yourself in Realities

Don't "oversell" your organization with swelled monetary projections and siphoned up marketing projections. Organizations that put resources into youthful organizations have been there, done that a couple of times and have a general comprehension of what's reasonable. In the event that you guarantee marketing projections two times as extensive as the opposition, for instance, they might well believe you're not being honest.

Be General and Direct

A decent marketable strategy shouldn't have more than 25 or 30 pages, and numerous great ones get started at 15 pages. Being excessively specialized and excessively distinct can add pointless duplication to your field-tested strategy and hold perusers back from zeroing in on the main thing, similar to your organization's associations and how your item or administrations will sell in your market.

● Legal Considerations and Registration

There is no normalized method for enlisting your business the country over. Each state has its own principles with respect to enrollment, both of a business and of its name. By and large, the enrollment of a business includes a few stages, including enlisting the business as the suitable structure, enlisting a business name, enrolling for licenses and allowances that are essential both inside the business and in the material wards, and enlisting with charge specialists.

The design that you pick during the arrangement of the business will direct, to a limited extent, the kinds of enrollment that should be finished.

Picking Your State

At the point when your business is a LLC or a partnership, it is important to pick the state where you will document desk work to enlist your business. A partnership registers to make a legitimate element that is discrete from the singular proprietors or investors of the business and to safeguard the proprietors from lawful obligation. Most enterprises consolidate in the state where the company intends to manage a large portion of its exchanges. There are sure states, like

Delaware, that offer great duty treatment, and a few enterprises like to consolidate in those states. To consolidate, the organization needs to record development archives with the Secretary of State's office.

Licenses and Allows

Organizations need to obtain any fundamental licenses or allow them to work. These can incorporate proficient licenses for specialists or grants connected with a self-start venture. They can likewise incorporate drafting licenses to guarantee that the business can be run in the ideal area.

Enlisting the Business Name

Your business structure will likewise decide if you want to enlist your business name. In the event that you are working with sole ownership under your own name, you would likely not have to enlist the name. Nonetheless, on the off chance that you are beginning a restricted organization, LLC, or enterprise, or on the other hand assuming that you are carrying on with work under a made up name, the circumstance is more confounded. In addition to other things, you might need to consider whether the name that you are picking has been reserved, since you will need to keep away from brand name encroachment. Nonetheless, in many states, you are enlisting your name when you document articles of joining or association, or an assertion of restricted organization with the state recording office, and different organizations can not utilize the name once you record.

Individuals selling items or administrations under a name other than their own should document a made up name explanation or expected name endorsement. In many states, these reports can be recorded with the Secretary of State or Division of Partnerships, yet you ought to actually look at your own state's standards. Each state has its own prerequisites for made up or expected business names, however by and large, most banks won't open a record under the business name without confirmation of enlistment, and you can likewise not implement contracts endorsed under the imaginary business name without enrolling.

Brand name Insurance

While there is no lawful necessity to do as such, you can likewise enroll your business name with the U.S. Patent and Brand name Office and with your state as a brand name to give an additional layer of insurance. It tends to be destructive to have your business' image mistook for another business' image. Enlisting a brand name safeguards a business in the event that an alternate business later proposes a similar business name or a confusingly comparative name.

Charge Enlistment

Whether you have workers or any accomplices will direct what you want to do regarding charge enrollment. Individuals who work with sole ownership will document the business' charges as private expenses and may involve a Government managed retirement number to deal with monetary issues for the business. Notwithstanding, in the event that you have a business with representatives, no matter what the construction of the business, you should apply for government and state charge IDs. You will likewise have to make good on quarterly assessed charges and perhaps gather deals.

Chapter 3:Define

• Defining Your Business Idea and Unique Value Proposition

A unique value proposition (UVP) is your approach to educating potential clients concerning the advantages your business gives. UVP might allude to a whole association, a specific item or administration, or client accounts.

Why is a value proposition important?

An incentive is the most important thing in the world of your business. It underlies the items and administrations your image offers, characterizes your promoting technique and situating, etc.

The essential undertaking of an UVP is to clear up for your clients why working with you or utilizing your item is the best choice. Without it, your customer base is probably not going to sort out how your item satisfies their requirements and why they ought to pick it.

One more capability of an incentive is to separate your image from rivals. Regardless of whether you offer off-the-rack items, you want to make them hang out in succession of comparable things, and an unmistakable UVP assists you with getting it done.

In this way, a special incentive makes your image unique and charming to clients. Notwithstanding, there are a few additional significant advantages this idea gives your business. Peruse on to investigate them.

Benefits of a Value Proposition

An offer is a thing that characterizes your business, advancement technique, and outcome on the lookout. Here are the primary benefits a very much planned UVP can bring your business:

Clear correspondence: An incentive assists you with making a decent proposal to your clients. Clearness drives more possibilities at the top phases of the business channel and allows you to support income.

More excellent leads: Over portion of planned clients bungle your organization. An incentive assists you with accomplishing practically 100 percent crossover between your expected purchasers' requirements and the issues your item handles. It drives higher change rates and saves exertion enjoyed on working with an inadmissible customer base.

Further developed commitment: At the point when your clients' qualities coordinate with your organization's, it prompts expanded commitment with your image, items, and administrations.

Bound together informing: An UVP explains your proposition and convenience both for clients and workers. In this manner, you should rest assured that everybody sends similar qualities across various correspondence channels - your site, points of arrival, online entertainment pages, and the sky's the limit from there.

Coherent correspondence, great leads, high commitment rates, and steady informing influence your business and monetary measurements emphatically. Ultimately, you'll get an expansion in consumer loyalty, activity proficiency, return for money invested, etc. All things considered, few out of every odd UVP can work like enchantment for your business.

What makes an effective value proposition?

An intricate incitement can change the game for your image. Notwithstanding, to negotiate viability, your UVP ought to fit the accompanying models:

- **limpidness**: An incitement should be egregious and straightforward from the onset.

- **swiftness:** An implicit customer ought to spend just a few seconds to get their head around your incitement.

- **Advantage:** A decent incitement separates your association from rivals.

- **reliableness:** An incitement ought to allude to substantial issues a customer will get from your item or administration.

- **Believability:** ensure you can convey the worth you've guaranteed. In any case, your business comes down and out, as guests rush to perceive duplicity and advise others.

- **A redundant recommendation:** keep down from creation and void expressions while creating your incitement. Expressions like" astounding item" look bad to shoppers and repulse them. For an analogous explanation, you ought to avoid" stylish" and different samples- except if you can demonstrate that you truly reserve the honor to use them — when you're the reasonable business colonist in a specialty.

How to produce a value proposition

There's an algorithm to help you form a value proposition:

Allude to your image personality

Assuming your business' central thing is dubious or ineffectively stated, you are presumably not going to make a coherent incitement. To find and accessible your image's personality, answer the accompanying inquiries:

- For what reason does your image live?
- How would you like to shape what is in store?
- How might you make that future?
- What norms uphold your way of carrying?

For illustration, on the off chance that you're fostering a reasonable style brand, you can respond to these inquiries like this

" Mass- request brands produce transitory garments, exhausting regular means, and jumbling up the Earth. We've an optional methodology. We use spare creation to bring out vestibules that endures longer. Our introductory beliefs areeco-kind disposition and top quality."

Fete your item's benefits

For this assignment, conceptualize every one of the advantages your item offers, including useful and close to home bones

. As similar, you can make reference to unequivocal rates your item has, as well as the passions it achieves in your guests. For a supportable design brand, you might name superior grade, exemplary styles, and the pride an individual feels when they wear innocently created garments.

Just sit back and relax assuming the program is exorbitantly lengthy, you'll estimate the advantages and cross out the meaningless latterly. When the rundown is set, attempt to sort out what regard every one of the benefits brings to a customer. It could be time investment finances or cost, aiding with driving the way of life they need to,etc.

Coordinate your benefits with customer's enterprises

To ensure your incitement will arrive at your ideal, make a rundown out of issues your implicit guests face. Take just those that connect with your item. For illustration, your possibilities might battle to track down sturdy vesture or can not bear to get it from utmost reasonable design brands.

To describe these issues, make a purchaser persona- follow our primer to produce a conceivable customer profile. To get a more clear picture, lead exploration- read web-grounded entertainment and online gatherings where your implicit purchasers invest energy and distinguish the issues they examine. You may likewise direct outside and out overviews of your ongoing guests.

Focus on the significance of purchasers' enterprises in the rundown and coordinate them with your advantages. Center around the main issues your implicit purchasers face. This step is a veterinarian to conduct your incitement meetly. Flash back that guests need to hear how your item takes care of their enterprises, not a rundown of highlights.

Make sense of what makes you the stylish supplier of significant worth

Offer suggests separation from contenders. In this way, after you've made a rundown of your item benefits and coordinated it with the customer issues, direct a contender exploration. Take a gander at what they offer guests and distinguish their impulses. This will help you with understanding how to figure out your UVP in a way that beats your opponents.

To get effects right, center around the distinctions between what your rivals propose and what you can offer. For illustration, assuming an opponent style brand makes expensive garments, point that you give a less precious other option. Emphasize contrasts that make your business stick out.

Resolve your novel offer

At this point, you have mindfulness about your image, character, item benefits, and their incentive for possible clients, as well as contrasts among you and your rivals. With this data available, outline your offer in one short sentence. Attempt different components and perceive how they cooperate.

At the outset, you can think of a few assertions. Offer choices for a practical design brand might seem like "We make moral style reasonable" or "We give excellent dress to a spotless future." Ensure all your UVP varieties are clear and succinct.

Part test and refine

In the event that you end up with a few offers, run A/B tests to figure out which variation performs best. The most ideal choice is to give a preliminary for offers that are fundamentally not quite the same as one another. Go for changes that emphasize different client issues or stress differentiating benefits.

To test incentives, you can send off a few renditions of presentation pages or lead reviews. Pose your clients these inquiries:

- What is your take on the varieties?
- For what reason do you lean toward certain choices over others?
- Do you have faith in our proposition?
- How would you figure out our suggestion?

Testing your offer assists you with understanding what explanations resound with your crowd. Additionally, on account of preliminaries you can refine these expressions to accomplish improved results.

Articulating your UVP obviously and briefly might be laborious work. To reduce the aggravation of expressing your qualities, you can utilize pre-planned equations.

Value Proposition Tips

The hypothesis permits you to make a general arrangement for finishing things, however a training makes you think of the best arrangements. Accordingly, we've picked favorable tips to assist you with supporting the adequacy of your incentive.

- **Structure your UVP as soon as could really be expected:** The prior you characterize your offer, the sooner you can profit from it. Even better, with a prepared to-utilize proclamation, you can begin further developing it immediately by testing. Such UVP preliminaries permit you to address your crowd's agonies and expectations all the more unequivocally and drive improved results.

- **Test values before proclamations:** Some of the time offers don't perform well in tests. To track down the explanation, look at suspicions about the crowd's agonies and values prior to testing UVP articulations. Make a little center gathering and look at their convictions about your speculations.

- **Adjust your offer every once in a while:** As time passes quickly, your interest group might change their inclinations and values. A recognizable incentive may not reverberate with the new client convictions as well as it used to. Consequently, testing and refining your offer on occasion is really smart.

• Identifying Target Markets and Niches

The main part of setting up a fruitful business is knowing your optimal clients inside your particular specialty.

Your main interest group is the gathering who fall inside a comparable segment with shared interests, values and convictions. At the point when you are clear about your particular specialty, recognizing your main interest group will be a lot more straightforward. When you know who your main interest group is, you can then carry out your advertising, including the course of your substance and item advancement. In this manner, picking a specialty ought to never be undervalued.

Recognize your enthusiasm and abilities

The most ideal way to pick a specialty is to initially settle on what you appreciate and what you are great at. Along these lines, you will actually want to adapt your energy and your expertise. With the two key variables joined, you will actually want to construct areas of strength for your business. Accomplishing something that you are enthusiastic about will keep you spurred over the long haul, since you are accomplishing something that you love. This will be the fundamental drive that pushes you along at whatever point you want to surrender. In the event that you are accomplishing something that you detest, you have a higher possibility of stopping as it will be more challenging to remain persuaded.

At the point when you additionally pick something that you love, you'll normally be great at it. At the point when you're great at what you love to do, you can tackle issues in that specific market, since you are utilizing a range of abilities that you as of now have.

Recognize your main interest group's concerns

Building a productive business is tied in with figuring out the issues and wants of your main interest group and having the option to overcome any barrier to assist them with getting to where they need to be. To take care of their concerns, you should initially know about the issues that they are confronting.

So how do you have any idea about what kind of issues they are confronting? With the web readily available, we can undoubtedly look for catchphrases on Google to figure out what trouble spots our potential clients are confronting. Facebook gatherings and Quora are extraordinary stages to find the inquiries that individuals are posing. They are additionally ideal spots for statistical surveying. Investigate the conversations that are occurring and attempt to see what questions they are asking, alongside the issues they are confronting.

Research your opposition

It means a lot to know your opposition to genuinely comprehend where you stand so you can decide the productivity of the market. Understanding your rivals will empower you to recognize market holes and fill the hole. You'll get to lay out your novel incentive and decide if the market is oversaturated or not. Realizing your rivals will provide you with a thought of how to outclass them by concentrating on their assets and shortcomings. Contender examination and observing your exhibition will assist you with being exceptional with making enhancements en route.

Decide possible benefit

During your statistical surveying, you ought to have a thought of the benefit of your specialty as you accumulate data. Picking an evergreen industry is one method for guaranteeing that your business will be in a productive market. A few business sectors will quite often perform better compared to others since they are evergreen, and that truly intends that there is generally demand in those business sectors. You can direct statistical surveying utilizing Google Patterns to find moving themes and watchwords that are exceptionally looked at. It is essential to decide if the specialty you have picked has a need and whether individuals will pay for what you bring to the table.

Approve your thought

The last thing that you believe you should do prior to settling on your specialty is to approve your thought by running a test. You can utilize crowdfunding sites, for example, Kickstarter to approve your item thought and raise subsidies all the while. You can likewise make a greeting page on MailChimp and begin gathering drives just to find out how well the advancement turns out and whether the specialty that you pick has any interest. One fast method for doing that is by running a couple of paid promotions to guide clients to your greeting page and measure the presentation of your advertisements.

The most terrible thing that can happen is picking a specialty with low interest, enlisting your organization, and having your site going, just to understand that no one needs your items or administrations. These are botches that you can stay away from assuming you carry out this large number of steps prior to finishing your specialty and making things ready.

Lay out areas of strength

It might appear to be tiring to lead statistical surveying and contender examination, however every startup needs to construct areas of strength for a. It's critical to comprehend your rivals however much that your clients do so you can continually make upgrades in your advertising. At the point when that's what you do, you are fortifying your special incentive after some time and making a brand that sticks out.

Chapter 4:Learn

• Consistent information and Expertise Improvement

Consistent information is the nonstop augmentation of data and scopes of limits. With felicitations to finish improvement in the functioning territory, it's connected to developing new limits and data, while likewise supporting what has been as of late understood.

Meaning of consistent information

Consistent information is basic in the current dynamic and snappily creating world.

As endeavors and innovations constantly advance, individuals and gatherings who focus on consistent information gain an advantage and adaptability basic for progress.

Embracing an endless information standpoint energizes individual and master improvement, allowing individuals to acquire new limits, stay huge in their fields, and correct their decisive reasoning chops.

Seven different ways consistent information will help you

Data is as of now promptly accessible. Those not making activity of this entryway will remain where they are, their abilities lessening in its importance. These seven benefits should be reason enough no way to stop information.

1. Remain huge

Make an effort not to be deserted. Promise you stay material to your diligence by keeping awake with the rearmost with designs and adjusting your scope of limits. To work effectively among this snappily influencing production of creation, you truly need to learn new merchandise to remain huge.

2. Prepare for the unlooked-for

Profound confirmed information will assist you with adjusting to unlooked-for changes, for example, losing your business and depending upon new abilities to search for a good work. By pacing to learn, you'll even more really escape your standard scope of commonality and seek after on new position open entryways.

3. Assist you with profiling

Exactly when you're consistently learning, you'll proceed to correct and fill in your livelihood and start to get propositions from partners and chiefs. The chances are great that you'll turn occupations on various events generally through your life and you need to secure new abilities to as prerequisites be adjusted.

4. Expertise prompts sureness

Learning new products furnishes us with a vibe of accomplishment, which in like manner upholds our confidence in our own abilities. Likewise, you'll feel more set to take on challenges and test new endeavors.

5. Touches off new investigations

procuring new limits will uncover new entryways and help you with finding innovative solutions for issues. This could get you farther money.

6. Change your perspective

Steady information opens your mind and changes your insight by developing what you certainly know. The more you learn, the better you'll get at seeing farther sides of a comparative situation, abetting you with seeing even more significantly.

7. Offer visionary grace

Relentless information isn't just about you. Profound sleep with obtaining encourages your power limits which likewise, by then, changes over into developing durable information in others, by enabling them to pursue crisp preparation.

The best framework to continually find some new data

- Begin pouring by saving your time.
- Manufacture a relationship of go-to subject matter experts and get clarification on certain merchandise.
- Divert into a person from a participation associated with your work and begin putting together.
- Advance by showing someone else.
- Lead your own investigation and assessments.
- Go to the library and request the racks.
- See what's happening around you.
- Evaluate and consider what you've understood.
- Apply what you've understood.

- implies for learned
- Grasp magazines and online papers.
- Separate and gauge relevant assessments.
- Get involved with disseminations clear cut for your areas of interest.
- Make time to section with an overall relationship of distinctions practicing On the web Diversion and Dispatch.
- Go to instructive classes and events.
- Focus on web accounts and watch TED accounts.

• Statistical surveying and Contender Examination

Market investigation helps you with finding visitors for your business. Serious assessment helps you with making your business unique. Solidify them to find a high ground for your privately owned business.

Use demand investigation to find visitors

Measurable studying blends purchaser direct and monetary examples to attest and additionally foster your business permitted.

It's basic to appreciate your client base. Factual reviewing permits you to decrease bets for sure while your business is as yet a clue in your eye.

Gather part information to all the more promptly grasp astounding entryways and cutoff points for gaining visitors. This could streak back swarm data for age, wealth, family, interests, or whatever distinctively that is relevant for your business.

Likewise, by then, answer the going with requests to get a capable of your solicitation

- Demand: Is there a hankering for your thing or organization?
- Demand size: What number of singularities could be enthused about your gift?

- Monetary pointers: What's the compensation reach and business rate?

- Region: Where do your visitors reside and where could your business anytime reach?

- demand retention: What number of comparable decisions are presently open to visitors?

- Assessing: What do certain visitors pay for these different choices?

You will similarly have to remain uncertain of the latest confidential experience designs. It's basic to secure a sensation of the specific part of the general assiduity that will influence your advantages.

You can do factual reviewing, practicing being sources, or you can do the assessment yourself and go direct to customers.

Being sources can save you a lot of huge speculation, yet the information probably won't be too characterized for your group as you'd like. Use it to resolve questions that are both general and quantifiable, undifferentiated from assiduity designs, economics, and family profit.

Requesting buyers yourself can give you a nuanced appreciation from your specific vested party. However, direct assessment can be dreary and costly. Use it to address requests concerning your specific business or visitors, undifferentiated from reactions to your emblem, overhauls you could make to buying experience, and where visitors could go instead of your business.

Coming up next are several procedures you can use to do organize disquisition:

- Audits
- checks
- Focus social affairs
- Top to nethermost gatherings
- utilize serious assessment to find a solicitation advantage

Serious disquisition helps you with acquiring from affiliations vying for your potential visitors. This is essential to portraying a high ground that makes opportune pay.

Your serious assessment should fete your resistance by item immolation or organization and solicitation scrap. Gauge the coinciding paces of the Cunning scene

- Piece of the general assiduity
- Rates and shortfalls
- Your entryway to enter the solicitation
- The meaning of your goal solicitation to your adversaries
- Any deterrents that could disappoint you as you enter the solicitation
- Distorted or strengthening competitors who could affect your substance

Chapter 5:Experiment

• Embracing a Culture of Innovation

A culture of innovation is characterized as the aggregate outlook, values, convictions, and practices inside an association that encourage and uphold advancement. It is a climate where innovativeness, trial and error, and the quest for groundbreaking thoughts are supported and embraced. In a culture of development, people are engaged to think fundamentally, face challenges, and rock the boat to produce advancement arrangements and drive positive change.

Key qualities of a culture of innovation regularly include:

- **Liberality:** An eagerness to investigate additional opportunities and think about elective points of view.
- **Joint effort:** Empowering cross-utilitarian collaboration and the trading of thoughts to cultivate development.
- **Trial and error:** Establishing a climate that takes into account experimentation, gaining from disappointments, and emphasizing on thoughts.
- **Risk resilience:** Tolerating and, surprisingly, uplifting well balanced plans of action, understanding that advancement includes vulnerability.
- **Flexibility:** Being receptive to change, embracing innovation development and market elements, and adjusting methodologies appropriately.
- **Ceaseless picking up:** Esteeming progressing individual and expert turn of events, embracing a development

mentality, and supporting information sharing.

- **Steady initiative:** Pioneers who move and enable their groups, giving assets, independence, and a place of refuge for development.
- **Acknowledgment and reward:**Acknowledging and celebrating imaginative endeavors and results, boosting innovative reasoning and critical thinking.
- **Client centricity:** Putting clients at the focal point of advancement endeavors, input from clients is effectively looked for and coordinated into the development cycle.
- **Long haul center:** Perceiving that development is a nonstop cycle that requires supported exertion and speculation, instead of a one-time occasion.

• Implementing Agile Strategies and Prototyping

Grasping Lithe Standards:

Nimbleness in business includes embracing a bunch of rules that focus on adaptability, coordinated effort, and client criticism. Light-footed techniques include separating projects into more modest, reasonable errands, known as emphases or runs. This iterative methodology takes into consideration consistent reassessment and variation, guaranteeing that the end result lines up with advancing necessities and market elements.

Iterative Advancement with Runs:

Runs are the heartbeat of spry systems. These short, engaged times of work include arranging, executing, and investigating undertakings. By working in runs, your group can quickly adjust to changes, answer arising difficulties, and coordinate client criticism successfully. The iterative idea of runs guarantees that your task develops in a state of harmony with true requests.

Client Driven Prototyping:

Prototyping is the extension among conceptualization and execution. As opposed to sitting tight for a completely evolved item, make models — downsized variants that permit you to test ideas, assemble criticism, and refine your contribution. A client driven way to deal with prototyping guarantees that your end result reverberates with the requirements and inclinations of your interest group.

Bomb Quick, Learn Quicker:

Dexterous procedures and prototyping share a typical way of thinking: the significance of learning through activity. Embrace the idea of "bomb quick, learn quicker." By rapidly recognizing what doesn't work, you gain important experiences that guide your subsequent stages. This approach limits the gamble of putting time and assets toward a path that might require change.

Empowering Cross-Useful Joint effort:

Light-footed procedures blossom with joint effort. Separate storehouses inside your association, empowering cross-useful groups that unite different abilities and viewpoints. This cooperative methodology upgrades imagination, speeds up critical thinking, and guarantees that tasks benefit from a scope of skill.

Adjusting to Changing Economic situations:

The business scene is steadily developing, and dexterous systems are intended to flourish in such circumstances. By consistently reconsidering needs, adjusting to advertise moves, and answering client criticism, your business stays deft and responsive. This flexibility is a critical resource in a climate where change is the main consistent.

Ceaseless Improvement:

Executing light-footed systems and prototyping is definitely not a one-time exertion yet a nonstop excursion. Consistently survey and consider your cycles, looking for amazing open doors for development. The capacity to gain from every emphasis, refine your strategies, and execute improvements positions your business in a direction of supported development and advancement.

In this present reality where change is unavoidable, executing coordinated procedures and prototyping turns into a compass for enterprising achievement. These powerful instruments engage you to explore vulnerability with certainty, answer developing business sector elements, and change your thoughts into effective, client driven advancements.

Chapter 6:Hard Work

In the embroidery of business ventures, difficult work is the string that meshes dreams into the real world. This part investigates the meaning of difficult work — the tenacious exertion, tirelessness, and responsibility that structure the foundation of any effective enterprising excursion.

Responsibility Past Solace:

Difficult work is a demonstration of your responsibility. It implies pushing past the limits of solace and embracing the difficulties that come your direction. It's a day to day choice to empty your energy into your endeavor, in any event, when the way appears to be steep and the result unsure.

Tirelessness Even with Difficulties:

Business venture is an excursion weighed down with difficulties. Difficult work is the enduring steadiness to handle these difficulties head-on. It's tied in with seeing misfortunes not as barriers but rather as any open doors to learn, change, and arise more grounded on the opposite side.

Reliable Exertion Yields Results:

Progress in business is many times a consequence of reliable, devoted exertion. It's the amount of little, day to day activities that, over the long haul, collect into critical advancement. Difficult work is the obligation to appear, placing in the hours, and making progress toward your objectives, regardless of how steady.

Building a strong work ethic:

At the center of difficult work are areas of strength for an ethic. It's tied in with imparting discipline in your daily practice, dealing with your time successfully, and focusing on errands in light of their effect. A hearty hard working attitude upgrades efficiency as well as sets the establishment for long haul achievement.

Exceeding all expectations:

Difficult work frequently implies blowing away what is generally anticipated. It's the additional mile — the extra exertion that recognizes your endeavor from the rest. Whether it's conveying uncommon client care, refining your items resolutely, or putting resources into consistent improvement, exceeding everyone's expectations turns into a sign of your pioneering venture.

Embracing Penances for Progress:

The way of difficult work now and again includes making penances. It could mean late evenings, missed get-togethers, or renouncing prompt satisfaction for the drawn out vision. Business visionaries who comprehend the craft of key penance end up better situated for supported achievement.

Developing a Development Mentality:

Difficult work isn't just about the actual exertion; it's likewise a mentality. Business visionaries with a development outlook consider difficulties to be potential chances to learn and develop. They view difficult work not as a weight but rather as an interest in their own and proficient turn of events.

In the orchestra of business ventures, difficult work is the relentless beat that drives your process forward. It's the monotonous routine, the perspiration value, and the refusal to be hindered by impediments. As you explore the difficulties and wins of your innovative way, let difficult work be the song that reverberates with the flexibility and assurance that characterize your prosperity.

Chapter 7: How to Finance a Business

Getting sufficient subsidizing for your business can be challenging. Notwithstanding, it's memorable that going into business is a huge venture that ought to be given a proper time frame to succeed.

Frequently, new organizations need to raise subsidizing rapidly and productively to appropriately develop and flourish in their given market, however it tends to be challenging to stick to different loaning prerequisites without existing monetary data. Notwithstanding these difficulties, there are different monetary assets that can assist you with getting your business going.

Assess STARTUP Expenses AND Costs

Prior to choosing how to back your business, decide how much cash you expect to require for startup expenses and normal costs. Whether you run a blocks and concrete or online business, think about the accompanying while considering costs:

- Licenses and allows
- Brand names, copyrights, or licenses for your image and items
- Business protection
- Legitimate or bookkeeping help
- Lease and utilities (for physical organizations)
- Hardware expected for creation
- Site stages
- Promoting materials (both print and computerized)
- Delivering supplies

- Memberships to content administration frameworks and deals or showcasing stages
- Statistical surveying

• Funding Options: Bootstrapping, Loans, Investors

Setting out on the exhilarating ride of business frequently requires a touch of monetary enchantment. We should unload the various ways you can subsidize your fantasies - whether you're handling your own problems, thumping on the bank's entryway for a credit, or cozying up to likely financial backers.

1. Bootstrapping: The Do-It-Yourself Approach

Bootstrapping is like building a sandcastle with your own hands. It's utilizing your investment funds or the cash your business makes to subsidize its development. It's the gradual way, offering you the opportunity to call the chances however requesting a spot of persistence.

Potential gain:

- You're the skipper of your boat.
- No obligations or offering benefits to pariahs.
- Trains you to be a monetary ninja.

Drawback:

- Development could take a piece longer.

- Your own investment funds are on the line.
- Requires a touch of monetary shuffling.

2. Credits: Getting Somewhat Wizardry

Credits resemble getting a touch of monetary stardust to get things going. You can thump on the bank's entryway or investigate other loaning choices. It's a quicker method for getting cash, yet it accompanies the obligation to repay it with a touch of extra.

Potential gain:

- Fast admittance to cash.
- You keep control of your business.
- Reimbursement terms are spread out.

Drawback:

- Your record as a consumer needs to sparkle.

- Adds obligation to your business' shoulders.
- Interest installments are important for the arrangement.

3. Financial backers: Tracking down a Monetary Partner

Financial backers resemble divine helpers - they sprinkle their wizardry (cash) on your business in return for a slice of the pie. It's an organization where they share your fantasies and, ideally, your prosperity.

Potential gain:

- A heap of money for fast development.
- Experienced financial backers bring insight.
- Shared chances and, preferably, a guide in your corner.

Drawback:

- You surrender a cut of possession.
- Your say might get weakened.
- Financial backers anticipate a decent return.

Picking Your Monetary Experience:

The mystery ingredient frequently lies in blending these choices. Perhaps start with a touch of bootstrapping, add a sprinkle of credits for a fast lift, and in the event that your fantasies are basically as large as the sky, welcome financial backers to the party. Creating a monetary arrangement moves to the musicality of your business objectives and chance hunger.

In this way, whether you're taking the panoramic detour of bootstrapping, hitching a ride on a credit, or uniting with financial backers, the key is to pick the blend that feels ideal for your pioneering venture. All things considered, each fantasy needs a touch of monetary sorcery to take flight really.

• Budgeting and Financial Planning

In the terrific arrangement of business ventures, planning and monetary arranging are the guides directing each monetary note. This part investigates the craftsmanship and significance of planning — making a guide for your cash — and monetary preparation — decisively controlling your business toward monetary achievement.

1. Making a Financial plan: The Writer's Score

Planning resembles making a melodic score for your business — it gives construction, bearing, and congruity. Start by posting your pay sources and ordering costs. Allot reserves decisively to regions like activities, advertising, and development drives. A very much created spending plan turns into the directing tune that keeps your monetary ensemble on target.

Key Planning Parts:

Income Projections: Gauge your pay sources, considering deals, associations, or other income streams.

Fixed and Variable Costs: Sort costs that stay steady (lease, compensations) and those that vacillate (promoting, utilities).

Secret stash: Put away assets for unanticipated costs or potential open doors, going about as a security net for your business.

2. Monetary Preparation: Organizing Long haul Achievement

Monetary arranging is the guide's twirly doo, coordinating the drawn out musicality of your business. It includes laying out key monetary objectives, illustrating moves toward accomplishing them, and adjusting as your business develops. It's not just about enduring the monetary notes of today yet coordinating an ensemble of manageable achievement.

Components of Monetary Preparation:

Objective Setting: Characterize present moment and long haul monetary objectives, for example, income targets, productivity edges, or development plans.

Income The board: Screen your income to guarantee a good arrangement among pay and costs. Expect likely plunges and plan appropriately.

Obligation The board: On the off chance that your business has credits, devise an arrangement to decisively oversee and reimburse them.

Speculation System: Investigate amazing open doors to reinvest benefits for development, whether in showcasing, innovation, or growing your product offering.

3. Versatility and Adaptability: Orchestrating with Change

In the monetary orchestra of business ventures, flexibility is the way to remain on top of evolving elements. Routinely return to your financial plan and monetary arrangement, changing the notes as your business develops or economic situations shift. Adaptability permits you to blend with the startling and quickly jump all over new chances.

Tips for Adaptability:

Ordinary Audits: Lead intermittent surveys of your financial plan and monetary arrangement, guaranteeing they line up with current business real factors.

Situation Arranging: Expect various situations, for example, financial movements or industry changes, and have alternate courses of action set up.

Input Circles: Energize open correspondence inside your group to assemble bits of knowledge and adjust your monetary systems appropriately.

Planning and monetary arranging are not static organizations but rather unique arrangements that develop with your business. As you calibrate your monetary orchestra, recollect that each note adds to the agreeable progress of your pioneering venture. In this way, embrace the guide's job, refine your monetary score, and let your business play out a work of art of financial versatility and thriving.

Chapter 8:Acquiring New Customers

By procuring new clients, a business can build its income and overall revenues, which can then be reinvested to secure much more clients. This makes an upright pattern of development, where each new client assists with driving further growth.This part investigates the methodologies and strategies associated with contacting new clients, extending your crowd, and building enduring associations on the lookout.

• Effective Marketing Strategies

1. Exhaustive Statistical surveying: Enlightening the Scene

Prior to creating your advertising system, dig into the complexities of your market. Grasp your rivals, distinguish purchaser needs, and observe market patterns. This essential examination lays the preparation for designated and effective advertising efforts.

Steps in Statistical surveying:

- Contender Examination: Recognize qualities, shortcomings, and special selling points of contenders.
- Purchaser Conduct Study: Figure out the inclinations, propensities, and trouble spots of your interest group.

- Pattern Investigation: Remain sensitive to industry drifts that can illuminate your showcasing approach.

2. Characterize a Reasonable Incentive: Articulating Your Remarkable Contribution

Your incentive is the heartbeat of your showcasing procedure. Obviously convey what separates your item or administration and how it tends to the requirements of your interest group. A convincing incentive structures the core of powerful information.

- Parts of Major areas of strength for a Suggestion (Emphasis):
- Lucidity: Obviously state what your proposition is and why it is important.
- Separation: Feature what separates you from contenders.
- Client Driven: Spotlight on the advantages your clients gain.

3. Content Advertising Greatness: Recounting Your Image's Story

Content is the narrator that produces associations with your crowd. Foster top caliber, drawing in happiness that lines up with your image personality. Use blog entries, recordings, infographics, and different configurations to share important data, exhibit skill, and construct a local area around your image.

Viable Substance Showcasing Methodologies:

- Instructive Substance: Offer industry bits of knowledge, how-to guides, and enlightening substance.
- Visual Narrating: Utilize convincing visuals to convey your image account.
- Reliable Contributing to a blog: Routinely distribute blog entries to

lay out power and encourage commitment.

4. Web-based Entertainment Authority: Exploring the Advanced Scene

Web-based entertainment stages are the clamoring commercial centers of the computerized age. Tailor your way to deal with the inclinations of your interest group. Participate in discussions, share applicable substance, and influence the force of web-based entertainment publicizing to enhance your image reach.

Web-based Entertainment Best Practices:

- Crowd Division: Designer content to explicit crowd portions on every stage.
- Intuitive Substance: Empower crowd cooperation through surveys, tests, and conversations.

- Investigation Use: Use stage examination to refine your technique in view of execution measurements.

5. Force to be reckoned with Joint efforts: Intensifying Your Arrive at through Partnerships

Powerhouses hold the amplifier to immense crowds. Distinguish powerhouses whose values line up with your image and work together on crusades. Powerhouse promoting can enhance your compass, construct validity, and make true associations with your interest group.

Steps in Powerhouse Coordinated effort:

- Examination and Choice: Distinguish powerhouses pertinent to your industry and target segment.

- Valid Associations: Look for powerhouses who legitimately line up with your image values.
- Cooperative Missions: Plan joint missions that reverberate with the powerhouse's crowd.

6. Email Showcasing Accuracy: Sustaining Long haul Connections

Email showcasing stays an amazing asset for supporting client connections. Foster designated email crusades that convey esteem, customized suggestions, and restrictive offers. Email mechanization can smooth out correspondence and give a predictable brand insight.

Key Components of Powerful Email Promoting:

- Division: Designer messages in view of client inclinations and ways of behaving.
- Personalization: Address clients by name and redo content for significance.
- Computerization: Carry out mechanized work processes for customized, convenient communications.

7. Measurements Checking and Variation: Refining Your Showcasing Ensemble

The progress of your advertising procedures lies in information bits of knowledge. Consistently screen key execution markers (KPIs) to measure the adequacy of your missions. Investigate change rates, client obtaining cost, and commitment measurements. Utilize this information to adjust and refine your promoting procedures for persistent improvement.

Basic Showcasing Measurements:

- Transformation Rates: Measure the level of leads that proselyte into clients.
- Client Obtaining Cost (CAC): Assess the expense of gaining another client.
- Commitment Measurements: Track likes, offers, remarks, and different marks of crowd connection.

Compelling advertising techniques are not static outlines but rather authentic plans that develop with your business and the market. By directing exhaustive exploration, characterizing a convincing offer, utilizing content showcasing, dominating virtual entertainment, working together with powerhouses, carrying out email accuracy, and embracing information driven transformation, you organize a promoting ensemble that reverberates with your crowd and impels your image toward supported progress in the cutthroat scene of business.

● Customer Relationship Management

A customer relationship management (CRM) arrangement assists you with tracking down new clients, winning their business, and keeping them cheerful by coordinating client and prospect data such that assists you assemble more grounded associations with them and develop your business quicker. CRM frameworks start by gathering a client's site, email, phone, web-based entertainment information, from there, the sky's the limit, across different sources and channels. It might likewise consequently pull in other data, like late news about the organization's action, and it can store individual subtleties, like a client's very own inclinations on correspondences. The CRM device coordinates this data to provide you with a total record of people and organizations in general, so you can more readily grasp your relationship over the long haul.

Advantages of CRM

A CRM framework helps organizations put together and unify their data on clients, taking into consideration simpler access and client care. Organizations use CRM frameworks to streamline deals and showcasing and further develop client maintenance. Information investigation is likewise a lot simpler, where organizations can follow the progress of different tasks or missions, distinguish patterns, construe affiliations, and make outwardly instinctive information dashboards.

Clients appreciate better help and are bound to report higher fulfillment accordingly. Client communications including grumblings are put away and can be handily reviewed so clients don't need to rehash the same thing continually.

Sorts of CRM

Today, numerous thorough CRM stages incorporate all pieces of the client relationship the business might have. Nonetheless, some CRMs are as yet intended to focus on a particular part of it:

- Deals CRM: to drive deals and increment the pipeline of new clients and possibilities. Accentuation is put on the deals cycle from following prompts shutting bargains.

- Advertising CRM: to fabricate, robotize, and track showcasing efforts (particularly on the web or by means of email), including distinguishing designated client sections. These CRMs give continuous measurements and can utilize A/B testing to enhance methodologies.
- Administration CRM: incorporated committed client care support with deals and showcasing. Frequently includes various contact focuses including responsive internet based visit, versatile, email, and virtual entertainment.
- Cooperative CRM: supports the sharing of client information across business portions and among groups to further develop proficiency and correspondence and work flawlessly together.

- Independent venture CRM: upgraded for more modest organizations with less clients to give those clients the most ideal experience. These frameworks are in many cases a lot less complex, natural, and more affordable to carry out than big business CRM.

Chapter 9:Online Business

In the period of computerized availability, sending off and growing a web-based business opens ways to tremendous open doors. This part investigates the complexities of laying out and flourishing in the domain of online business ventures, where the computerized skyline turns into the material for development, reach, and success.

In the far reaching domain of online business, the critical lies in essential preparation, a vigorous web-based presence, powerful online business stages, computerized promoting dominance, secure exchanges, client support greatness, and information driven refinement. By exploring the computerized skyline with a very much created plan and utilizing the devices accessible, your web-based business can get by as well as flourish in the serious and steadily developing scene of web based business.

• Leveraging the Power of the Internet

1. Computerized Presence: The Doorway to Worldwide Reach

Laying out a vigorous computerized presence is the doorway to a worldwide crowd. Make a very much planned site that grandstands your items or administrations as well as recounts your image story. Influence web-based entertainment stages to draw in with your crowd, construct a local area, and enhance your arrival at past geological limits.

Basics for a Solid Computerized Presence:

- Proficient Site: Specialty an easy to use and outwardly engaging site.
- Virtual Entertainment Commitment: Effectively partake in discussions on stages applicable to your crowd.

- Steady Marking: Guarantee a durable brand personality across every single computerized channel.

2. Internet business Development: From Neighborhood to Worldwide Business sectors

The web has upset trade, empowering organizations, everything being equal, to rise above neighborhood constraints. Embrace web based business stages and online commercial centers to sell items as well as tap into an immense pool of potential clients around the world. Redo your methodology in view of the idea of your business, whether it's specialty items or a different stock.

Systems for Worldwide Internet business Achievement:

- Confinement: Designer your substance and promote techniques to resonate with assorted crowds.
- Global Delivery: Offer dependable and practical transportation choices.
- Multilingual Help: Give client assistance in different dialects for upgraded openness.

3. Advanced Advertising Dominance: Exploring the Internet based Landscape

Advanced promoting is the compass that directs your image through the perplexing scene of the web. Execute website streamlining (Web optimization) methodologies to upgrade perceivability, influence paid promoting for designated reach, and bridle the force of content advertising to lay out thought authority in your industry.

Compelling Advanced Promoting Strategies:

- Web optimization Advancement: Further develop your site's web crawler positioning for expanded perceivability.

- Pay-Per-Snap (PPC) Publicizing: Target explicit socioeconomics with paid advertisements.
- Powerhouse Coordinated efforts: Cooperate with powerhouses to legitimately extend your span.

4. Information Driven Direction: Enlightening the Way ahead

The web creates an abundance of information that can be a directing light for business visionaries. Influence examination instruments to acquire bits of knowledge into client conduct, site execution, and the adequacy of advertising efforts. Information driven independent direction empowers you to emphasize on techniques, advance client encounters, and remain in front of market patterns.

Key Information Measurements for Vital Knowledge:

- Client Commitment: Screen site corporations, for example, time spent on pages and navigate rates.
- Change Rates: Track the level of site guests who become clients.
- Online Entertainment Examination: Investigate measurements like likes, offers, and remarks for crowd commitment.

5. Network protection Carefulness: Defending Advanced Resources

As the web opens roads for development, it likewise presents network safety challenges. Focus on the security of your web-based resources, client data, and conditional information. Carry out secure installment doors, routinely update programming, and teach your group on network safety best practices to strengthen your computerized fort.

Network protection Best Practices:

- Secure Installment Doors: Pick trustworthy and secure stages for monetary exchanges.

- Standard Programming Updates: Keep every single advanced apparatus and stages refreshed to fix weaknesses.

- Representative Preparation: Teach your group on perceiving and forestalling network safety dangers.

6. Coordinated Transformation: Flourishing in the Unique Advanced Scene

The web scene is consistently developing, requesting deftness from business people. Embrace a versatile attitude, keep up to date with innovative progressions, and be available to investigate arising patterns.

Whether it's embracing new specialized devices, incorporating increased reality into your client experience, or profiting by the ascent of voice search, nimbleness positions your business for supported significance.

Procedures for Lithe Variation:

- Persistent Learning: Remain informed about industry patterns and mechanical progressions.
- Client Input Reconciliation: Use client criticism to recognize regions for development and advancement.
- Trial and error: Be available to attempt new devices, stages, and

techniques to improve your computerized presence.

7. Local area Building: Cultivating Advanced Associations

The web isn't simply a commercial center; it's a local area center point. Cultivate associations with your crowd by effectively partaking in web-based networks, discussions, and online entertainment bunches applicable to your industry. Connect truly, share significant bits of knowledge, and fabricate connections that stretch out past conditional associations.

Local area Building Procedures:

- Commitment Stages: Take part in pertinent web-based discussions, gatherings, or networks.
- Content Sharing: Offer industry experiences, tips, and significant substance to lay out power.
- Client Appreciation: Recognize and value your computerized local area for their help.

Utilizing the force of the web isn't simply about laying out an internet based presence yet about decisively exploring the advanced territory to open development, encourage worldwide associations, and position your business at the front line of the computerized time. By embracing the amazing open doors introduced by the web, business visionaries can make due as well as flourish in the always growing advanced scene.

E-commerce Strategies and Digital Presence

1. Thorough Statistical surveying: Graphing Your Internet business Course

Prior to sending off your web based business adventure, leave on exhaustive statistical surveying. Grasp your interest group, examine contenders, and distinguish market patterns. This preparation shapes the establishment for key direction and guarantees your web based business technique lines up with market requests.

Key Parts of Internet business Statistical surveying:

- Crowd Division: Distinguish and grasp various portions of your interest group.
- Contender Investigation: Survey qualities, shortcomings, and interesting selling recommendations of contenders.
- Pattern Recognizable proof: Keep up to date with industry patterns molding the web based business scene.

2. Easy to understand Internet business Site: The Advanced Retail facade

Your online business site fills in as the virtual retail facade, affecting the client's insight and buy choices. Plan an easy to use and outwardly engaging site that focuses on simplicity of route. Guarantee consistent combination of item pages, secure checkout processes, and responsive plan for portable clients.

Components of a Successful Web based business Site:

- Instinctive Route: Improve on the client venture from item revelation to checkout.
- Top notch Symbolism: Feature items with clear, high-goal pictures.
- Secure Checkout: Execute secure installment doors to fabricate entrust with clients.

3. Portable Improvement: Catching the Versatile Customer

With a huge part of web based shopping happening on cell phones, improving your internet business webpage for versatility is basic. Guarantee a responsive plan that adjusts consistently to different screen sizes. Smooth out the portable shopping experience, from item perusing to checkout, to take care of the developing versatile customer segment.

Portable Enhancement Best Practices:

- Responsive Plan: Guarantee your site capabilities consistently across various gadgets.
- Speedy Stacking Times: Streamline pictures and components for quicker stacking on portables.

- Proficient Checkout: Work on the portable checkout process for accommodation.

4. Website improvement (Search engine optimization): Lifting Perceivability

Improve the discoverability of your online business website through compelling Search engine optimization techniques. Enhance item depictions, meta labels, and pictures to further develop web index rankings. Catchphrase research and significant substance creation add to serious areas of strength for an establishment.

Web optimization Best Practices for Web based business:

- Catchphrase Enhancement: Consolidate significant watchwords in item titles, depictions, and meta labels.
- Quality Item Portrayals: Art novel, educational, and watchword rich item depictions.
- Picture Improvement: Utilize distinct record names and alt labels for item pictures.

5. Content Showcasing: Narrating and Commitment

Past selling items, influence content showcasing to recount your image story and draw in your crowd. Foster blog entries, item guides, and mixed media content that offer some benefit to your clients. Content promoting helps your Website optimization endeavors as well as lays out your image as an expert in the business.

Content Promoting Procedures for Web based business:

- Item Exhibits: Make recordings displaying item elements and advantages.
- The most effective method to Guides: Foster educational aides connected with your item or industry.
- Client Created Content: Urge clients to share their encounters through audits and tributes.

Chapter 10:Grow, Adapt, Innovate

• Scaling Your Business

Steers for how to scale a business

While examining how to scale a business, we're alluding to development techniques that line up with your business vision while dealing with the effect of development on your organization. The accompanying steers for how to result in a business offer a solid and feasible scaling procedure.

1. Know your motivation

Scaling a business depends on making client dedication, and zeroing in on representative devotion is the most ideal way to construct client faithfulness. At the point when your workers are blissful, they'll get the message out and pass on their energy for your organization. Workers are faithful when their motivation and values line up with their organization, and they feel their professions have a higher reason.

On the off chance that you don't begin with your "why" of starting a new business in any case, then figuring out how to scale a business is of restricted utility. Knowing your motivation and effectively conveying that to your group is the method for making them raving fanatics of your organization and naturally drive development.

2. Foster a business map

Most business people have a marketable strategy, yet have you pondered fostering a business map? A business map is a viable and extensive way to scale a business and meet its objectives. It additionally prompts you to ask essential inquiries like "what business would you say you are truly in?" and "for what reason did you get into this business in any case?"

Business maps challenge you to take a gander at where you came from, characterize your motivation for beginning the business and look forward: What's next for your business, and where does your organization in a perfect world wind up? Recording these objectives is an urgent piece of figuring out how to scale a business and will be a useful reference when challenges gain out of influence.

3. Amazing your item or administration

While zeroing in on monstrous development, numerous entrepreneurs neglect to guarantee that they offer a strong item or administration, frequently calculating that they'll fix the issue in the wake of getting more clients or conveyance. Be that as it may, in the event that you don't dispose of the bugs first, they'll deteriorate while scaling a business. Figuring out how to scale a business prior to seeking after development will set aside your cerebral pains and cash over the long haul.

The early long periods of your business are a chance to pay attention to input, track down issues and work on your contributions until they live up to your clients' assumptions. At the point when you make an item or administration of magnificent quality, numerous development issues will deal with themselves. Tending to first-cycle issues likewise assists you with expecting control while scaling your business, as you'll have a more profound comprehension of what you and your clients maintain and need your item or administration should be.

4. Make smart cycles and tasks

The most effective method to scale a business doesn't simply include becoming vertical and outward. It additionally implies guaranteeing the consistent capability of your inward cycles and activities. The last thing you want is to lose clients you've endeavored to secure due to a shortcoming in your framework.

While consummating processes, recollect that frameworks and cycles that worked in your organization's beginning phases may not deal with a greater scale. As you develop, you'll have to change processes, which is where versatility and adaptability become fundamental. The way to scaling a business and shaping a strong center is laying out a structure of what worked and kept your business chugging along as expected in the early years. As development happens, you can constantly enhance this center, yet it isn't not difficult to reproduce whenever you've developed beyond a specific level.

5. Lay out your group

It appears glaringly evident yet laying out major areas of strength for a will is essential for scaling a business. Fostering an adaptable supervisory group to develop with the organization is pivotal in figuring out how to scale a business.

However, your group isn't just about your workers. To scale a business economically, work on creating outer associations with providers, accomplices and other external associations that are important for your general development.

Furthermore, recall your client base, which is one more center colleague. Quite possibly the best thing about working a private venture is laying out close connections with your clients and giving them your desired insight from start to finish. The objective is consistently to make a raving fan who advocates for your image and helps scale your business by getting the message out.

Keep in mind, the local area you make around your developing business can reinforce your establishment, strength and influence. Having a strong organization is essential for the meaning of scaling a business, so set aside some margin to fabricate a group to move you into what's in store.

6. Realize when to designate

With a solid group, you ought to have sufficient trust to use significant undertakings so you can work "on" the business rather than "in" it. Notwithstanding, as an entrepreneur, you need to feel engaged with each part of your organization and may experience issues giving up in specific regions. Utilizing undertakings is a gigantic piece of figuring out how to scale a business. What are you doing that another person could deal with?

Try not to exchange your time for dollars. Your business must have the option to run itself and flourish in any event, when you're not there. Do this by tending to restricting convictions, for example, "assuming I need something done well, I need to do it without anyone else's help," and by laying out designation propensities that permit you to claim your time.

7. Assemble your image

Scaling a business requires realizing your identity as an organization: what could you at any point offer your clients? How would you contrast with the opposition? What do you have that no other person does? What are your greatest shortcomings? What makes you so strong? What is your message? How would you upset your industry?

It could require a long time to respond to these inquiries, so start with an essential system and work from that point. More modest organizations can change gears simpler than enormous partnerships, so assuming there's a requirement for another methodology, utilize that as a valuable chance to improve and adjust.

Keep in mind, your image will establish the vibe for your organization's way of life as you scale. It will set the norm for making your recruits and laying out the client experience you need. It will likewise affect promoting, deals and plan endeavors and impact the organization you become

8. Associate with your client

Why even bother with scaling a business on the off chance that it doesn't create steadfast clients? Making raving devotees of your item is basic to permitting your business to flourish in the midst of the rhythmic movement of consistently changing buyer inclinations. While scaling a business, you're in a hatching period where you can test ways to deal with building and keeping up with client connections and client-focused rehearses in each feature of your business. You believe each colleague should show compassion, regard and receptiveness to encourage a cooperative culture of development. From that point, everybody on staff can construct a compatibility with your clients, making associations that will assist your item with selling itself.

• Adapting to Market Changes

Market changes are unavoidable and can present huge difficulties for any business. Whether it is another contender, a change in client interest, a mechanical development, or an administrative update, market changes can upset your ongoing technique and execution. How might you adjust to showcase changes really and remain on top of things? Here are a few systems to assist you with settling on better choices in a powerful climate.

1. Examine the climate

The initial step to adjust to advertise changes is to know about them. You really want to examine the outer and inner climate routinely and methodically to distinguish the patterns, open doors, dangers, and holes that influence your business. You can utilize devices like SWOT examination, PESTEL investigation, Watchman's five powers, and client input to assemble significant data and experiences. By filtering the climate, you can expect the likely effects of market changes and get ready for them likewise.

2. Assess your choices

The second move toward adjusting to advertise changes is to assess your choices. You want to evaluate the upsides and downsides of various strategies in light of your objectives, assets, abilities, and dangers. You can utilize instruments, for example, choice networks, money saving advantage investigation, situation arranging, and hazard examination to analyze and focus on your choices. By assessing your choices, you can pursue educated and judicious choices that line up with your vision and values.

3. Explore and learn

The third move toward adjusting to advertise changes is to try and learn. You want to test your suspicions and speculations prior to carrying out them for a huge scope. You can utilize instruments, for example, prototyping, pilot testing, A/B testing, and input circles to explore different avenues regarding your thoughts and measure their outcomes. By testing and learning, you can approve your choices and further develop them in light of the information and criticism you gather.

4. Impart and team up

The fourth move toward adjusting to showcase changes is to impart and team up. You want to share your vision, objectives, plans, and assumptions with your partners, like your representatives, clients, accomplices, and providers. You likewise need to pay attention to their perspectives, ideas, and concerns and include them in the dynamic cycle. You can utilize devices like pamphlets, gatherings, studies, and virtual entertainment to impart and team up really. By conveying and teaming up, you can assemble trust, commitment, and responsibility among your partners and influence their different viewpoints and abilities.

5. Screen and change

The fifth move toward adjusting to advertise changes is to screen and change. You really want to keep tabs on your development and execution against your goals and pointers and assess the results and effects of your choices. You likewise should be adaptable and nimble to answer new changes and criticism and alter your choices as needs be. You can utilize apparatuses like dashboards, reports, reviews, and surveys to screen and change your choices. By observing and changing, you can guarantee that your choices are significant, successful, and maintainable in an evolving market.

6. Develop and separate

The 6th move toward adjusting to advertise changes is to improve and separate. You want to make an incentive for your clients and partners by offering novel arrangements that address their issues and assumptions. You additionally need to separate yourself from your rivals by featuring your assets and benefits. You can utilize apparatuses, for example, conceptualizing, plan thinking, and incentive to advance and separate your items, administrations, and cycles. By developing and separating, you can acquire an upper hand and a faithful client base in an evolving market.

• Fostering a Culture of Innovation

Innovative culture alludes to a working environment climate that upholds innovativeness, risk-taking, trial and error, straightforwardness, and persistent improvement inside an association. It cultivates a climate that urges workers to break new ground, rock the boat, and produce novel thoughts and answers for complex issues. It likewise sees disappointment as a chance to learn.

For what reason is innovation culture significant

The present high speed business climate expects associations to adjust consistently to changing economic situations. By empowering representatives to embrace a deft attitude and break new ground, you cultivate the advancement of novel thoughts, items, and administrations that meet developing client needs and inclinations.

An organization that develops a culture of development likewise drives representative commitment and maintenance. By having workers contribute their ideas, sees, and imaginative reasoning, they gain a feeling of direction and possession in what they do, which prompts higher inspiration. Furthermore, it can likewise assist with drawing in top ability, as workers are bound to be locked in and satisfied in a climate that esteems their commitments and energizes trial and error.

An association with a solid development culture is better prepared to adjust to changes on the lookout, remain in front of the opposition, and drive development and accomplishment over the long haul.

Seven hints on the best way to make a culture of innovation

1. Advance an open disappointment culture

In an organization with an open disappointment culture, workers are urged to be straightforward about missteps and disappointments: representatives are not condemned for committing errors yet rather are upheld and urged to gain from their disappointments. The accentuation is on distinguishing the main drivers of disappointments and utilizing that information to further develop cycles, items, or administrations.

An open disappointment culture advances a development outlook, where gaining from disappointments is seen as a fundamental stage in the way to progress. It likewise cultivates trust and cooperation among colleagues, as individuals feel open to conceding errors and requesting help unafraid of revenge. Eventually, an open disappointment culture assists associations with being more creative, versatile, and strong despite difficulties and vulnerabilities.

Embracing an open disappointment culture can be a huge shift for organizations, yet there are a few methodologies you can take to make this progress:

Support straightforwardness:

Chiefs and administrators can set a model by sharing their own disappointments and empowering others to do likewise. Making a place of refuge where representatives feel happy with conceding botches is pivotal to encouraging an open disappointment culture.

Reevaluate disappointment as a learning a potential open door:

Rather than rebuffing or scrutinizing representatives for committing errors, pioneers can underline the significance of gaining from disappointments. Urge representatives to ponder what turned out badly, distinguish the underlying drivers, and foster answers for forestall comparative errors later on.

Celebrate progress, not simply achievement:

Perceive and praise endeavors and headway made towards accomplishing objectives, regardless of whether they haven't yet been completely accomplished. This assists with cultivating a climate of ceaseless improvement and development as opposed to simply zeroing in on ultimate results.

Offer help and assets:

Guarantee that workers have the assets they need to succeed, including preparing, apparatuses, and support from associates. Additionally, give valuable criticism to assist workers with gaining from their disappointments and work on their exhibition. Tragically, this point is ignored by many organizations.

Make disappointment noticeable:

Urge representatives to share their learnings and disappointments transparently, for instance, in group gatherings or through correspondence channels like pamphlets or web-based entertainment. This assists with normalizing disappointment as a characteristic piece of the educational experience and supports a climate of transparency and responsibility that cultivates development.

2. Lay out key partners on various levels

Key partners can give different points of view, experiences, and ability to illuminate advancement methodologies and drives. By including partners from various levels and divisions, associations can guarantee that advancement endeavors are lined up with business goals and needs and that they are coordinated into day to day tasks.

This approach likewise assists with cultivating cooperation, commitment, and possession around advancement, which is fundamental for supported achievement.

Enterprises can begin by recognizing and drawing in people who have areas of strength for an in and obligation to development.

Administrators can likewise make cross-practical groups to handle explicit advancement projects, uniting representatives with various abilities and mastery.

Organizations can lay out ordinary correspondence channels and arrangements for sharing thoughts, experiences, and best practices connected with advancement, making upsides of consistent learning and improvement.

This all can assist with animating the development of earth shattering thoughts.

3. Give spaces to unfurl inventiveness

To open inventiveness among representatives, they need a space where they can separate from their customary errands and that gives a home to deal with development themes.

Making a space that appears to be unique from the typical workplace (extravagant furnishings, extraordinary hardware) draws in representatives to consider some fresh possibilities and assists them with conceptualizing, sharing thoughts, and examination.

4. Carry out a go-to stage to open commitment and cooperation

To cultivate areas of strength for a culture, partnerships likewise ought to make computerized spaces for inside and outside partners to contribute and team up.

It's critical to affect individuals with the right abilities at each phase of the development interaction to build the possibilities of tracking down a decent arrangement. With expanding investment from inward groups and outer gatherings, for example, clients or accomplices, coordinated effort starts the rise of novel thoughts and improves existing ones.

Utilizing a stage that unifies all development tries encourages straightforwardness and works with interest across the enterprise. Gamification and correspondence highlights spur commitment and make it remunerating for individuals to reach out and contribute their thoughts.

The vital advantages of programming for driving innovation culture:

- Takes into account full straightforwardness of organization drives to upgrade arrangement towards key arranging goals and guarantee further developed prioritization and asset assignment.
- Providing a coordinated, secure cooperation space for thought age and progress toward advancement.
- Empowering information and report sharing, process improvement, and more proficient administration of development projects.

- Giving an organized means to assess data, thoughts, and drives for agreement in view of evaluated input.

- Checking cooperation to perceive and remunerate donors.

5. Give motivations

In the event that representatives don't completely partake in advancement exercises, one potential explanation could be that the impetus structure isn't adequately fulfilling. Prizes and motivators are an extraordinary method for spurring individuals to partake in development drives and to show them that their commitments offer some benefit to the organization. Motivators can be as rewards or advancements, for instance.

Impetuses can likewise cultivate cross-utilitarian cooperation when organizations boost groups to team up with others on a particular errand. This establishes a climate where thoughts are talked about more transparently with other colleagues, which can add to quicker and better critical thinking.

6. Cultivate outside-in development/open advancement

Open development has turned into a well known approach for organizations to use a bigger pool of thoughts and information, bringing about additional effective and imaginative items and administrations. When done really, open development practices can cultivate a climate of advancement inside the association.

Effective development requires a reconsidering of how worth is made, from ideation the entire way through to commercialization. Laying out open development rehearses that are advanced, incorporated, and simple to arrange and keep up with can altogether propel advancement achievement.

7. Lay out a deliberate interaction and backing straightforwardness

Associations should make an organized way to deal with development that is straightforward, methodical, and open to everybody in the organization. Knowing the course of ideation, assessment, and execution fabricates trust among representatives and further develops cooperation in advancement.

In addition, bits of knowledge and results must be conveyed straightforwardly all through the organization to keep key partners and workers informed.

Conclusion

Clearing the Way to Pioneering Greatness

In the rich embroidery of pioneering investigation introduced inside these pages, we've set out on an excursion directed by the insight and encounters shared by Vincent M. Lester. As we finish up this illuminating account, how about we embody the key bits of knowledge gathered and plant the seeds for proceeding with pioneering development.

• Summarizing Key Insights

Disclosing the Enterprising Embroidered artwork

Vincent's story has unfurled as a diverse embroidery, woven with strings of versatility, key intuition, and the dauntless soul of business. From the beginning of dares to enduring difficulties, the significance of flexibility and vital prescience has arisen as an ongoing idea. The meaning of encouraging a client driven approach, embracing development, and utilizing the force of the web remains as points of support supporting the innovative excursion.

The parts, whether diving into the subtleties of online business, showcasing ensembles, or the complexities of difficult work and monetary preparation, have on the whole laid out a far reaching representation of the innovative scene. Each brushstroke has added to the material of information, offering a mosaic of bits of knowledge that trying and prepared business people the same can draw motivation from.

● Encouraging Continued Entrepreneurial Growth

Supporting the Seeds of Development

As we close one part, the excursion of business is a ceaseless account, with open doors for development and advancement blooming not too far off. Vincent M. Lester's encounters act as a directing compass as well as fuel for the pioneering soul. The source of inspiration reverberates distinctly: keep on investigating, developing, and adjusting.

Pioneering development flourishes in the dirt of consistent learning and transformation. Vincent's encounters urge us to stay dexterous, embrace change, and view difficulties not as detours but rather as venturing stones to more prominent levels. The enterprising soul is a steadily advancing power, and chasing after greatness, one finds the seeds of advancement and versatility growing forward.

A Future Formed by Innovative Vision:

All in all, the bits of knowledge shared by Vincent M. Lester enlighten the way previously went as well as the future that lies ahead. The pages of this story hold the possibility to light enterprising sparkles, encourage development, and shape a future where organizations get by as well as flourish in the steadily changing scenes of business.

May the enterprising excursion ahead be loaded up with bold dreams, reasonable plans of action, and the steadfast assurance to change difficulties into open doors. As the drapery falls on this section, let it rise again on a future etched by the visionary undertakings of the people who hope against hope, enhance, and, most importantly, embrace the consistently developing excursion of business.

Review page

Dear Peruser,

I trust this message tracks down you feeling great. I'm writing to generously demand your smart survey of my late distributed book, "How to Start, Grow Your Own Business and Be Successful." Given your ability and adroit audits, your viewpoint would be amazingly significant to both me as a writer and likely perusers.

This book dives into the complexities of business, offering common sense exhortation on speculation like a business person, getting everything rolling, monetary procedures, online business, and significantly more. It is my earnest expectation that the substance ends up being both enlightening and rousing.

I grasp the requests on your time however would significantly see the value in your thought of this solicitation. Your criticism will without a doubt add to the continuous improvement of my work and help others in their enterprising undertakings.

Would it be a good idea for you to require any further subtleties or have explicit inquiries concerning the book, kindly go ahead and connect. Your readiness to share your contemplations is really valued.

Much obliged to you for thinking about my
solicitation.

Warm regards,

Vincent M. Lester

Author of "How to Start, Grow Your Own
Business and Be Successful"

www.ingramcontent.com/pod-product-compliance
Lightning Source LLC
Chambersburg PA
CBHW071039290526
45795CB00004B/1222